Primary School Chinese

with

Dalong, Xiaolong, Mike and Candy

Marcus Reoch and Anne Martin

This is the second book in a series of three books which encourage children to enjoy learning Chinese. There are ten chapters introducing new key topics and the language and characters learnt in the first book are revised and reinforced. Once again, each chapter contains a certificate, a Great Wall Challenge and stickers to further reinforce the key learning points. There is also a CD of the sound recordings at the back of the book.

Book 2 contains key sentence structures and a wide variety of games and puzzles to help children to practise Chinese. Clear, large character writing grids help children with character writing and there are games to make character learning fun. In addition, characters from Book 1 are reintroduced and built on to form sentences.

Marcus and Anne have written the book using the objectives of the Primary Languages Framework as a key reference tool. In addition, the core content follows the specifications for both MCTC® (Mandarin Chinese Teaching Certification) and The Independent Schools Examinations Board (ISEB) Level 1 Online Assessment (launched 2016).

The book also includes free access to **Primary School Chinese +** - a webp of games and competitions based on what they have already learnt. Please *www.primaryschoolchinese.com* for registration.

2

CONTENTS

Let's meet our 2 Chinese dragons again-
Dàlóng and Xiǎolóng!

Dàlóng
Big Dragon

Xiǎolóng
Little Dragon

Now let's meet their 2 friends again-
Mike and Candy!

Mike

Candy

 **Review: The 4 Chinese sounds!**

1st sound
is like
singing a song!

2nd sound
is like
climbing a ladder!

3rd sound
is like
being on a roller coaster!

4th sound
is like
falling over and saying 'ow'!

New words

shǒujī	mobile phone
tìxùshān	T-shirt
qiǎokèlì	chocolate

Good

xīn	new
měilì	beautiful
piányi	cheap

Bad

bù xīn	not new
bù měilì	not beautiful
bù piányi	not cheap

Nǐ mǎi shénme?	What are you buying?
Wǒ mǎi hànbǎobāo.	I am buying a hamburger.
Wǒ mǎi miàntiáo.	I am buying noodles.

What's in Dàlóng's shopping basket?

shǒujī **tìxùshān** **qiǎokèlì**

mobile phone   T-shirt   chocolate

What do you remember from Book 1? Complete the wordsearch below and make sure you find our **3** new words!

 màozi   **máoyī**

 wàzi   **bāo**

 kùzi   **qúnzi**

 jiákè   **xiézi**

 shǒujī   **shū**

 tìxùshān   **qiǎokèlì**

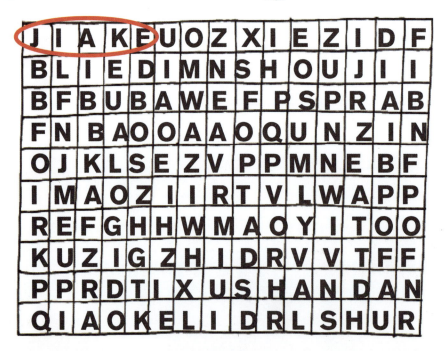

J	I	A	K	E	U	O	Z	X	I	E	Z	I	D	F
B	L	I	E	D	I	M	N	S	H	O	U	J	I	I
B	F	B	U	B	A	W	E	F	P	S	P	R	A	B
F	N	B	A	O	O	A	A	O	Q	U	N	Z	I	N
O	J	K	L	S	E	Z	V	P	P	M	N	E	B	F
I	M	A	O	Z	I	I	R	T	V	L	W	A	P	P
R	E	F	G	H	H	W	M	A	O	Y	I	T	O	O
K	U	Z	I	G	Z	H	I	D	R	V	V	T	F	F
P	P	R	D	T	I	X	U	S	H	A	N	D	A	N
Q	I	A	O	K	E	L	I	D	R	L	S	H	U	R

Let's learn some new words in Chinese!

xīn

new

měilì

beautiful

piányi

cheap

The mobile phone is...

Shǒujī hěn xīn.

The mobile phone is **new**.

The chocolate is...

Qiǎokèlì hěn piányi.

The chocolate is **cheap**.

Dàlóng's phone is new! Look at the three short sentences below and fill in the gaps with the missing Chinese words!

Dàlóng's phone is _**hěn**_ _**xīn**_. It is also _hěn xīn_.

Mike's T-shirt is _hěn měili_. It is also _hěn piànyi_.

Candy's chocolate is _hěn piànyi_. It is also _hěn xīn_.

How do you say **not** in Chinese?

bù xīn	**bù měilì**	**bù piányi**

not new	not beautiful	not cheap

 The T-shirt is...?

The jumper is...?

Tìxùshān bù piányi.

Máoyī bù měilì.

 The T-shirt is not cheap.

The jumper is not beautiful.

Xiǎolóng's socks are not new! Link the pictures to the words on the right and complete the sentences below in English!

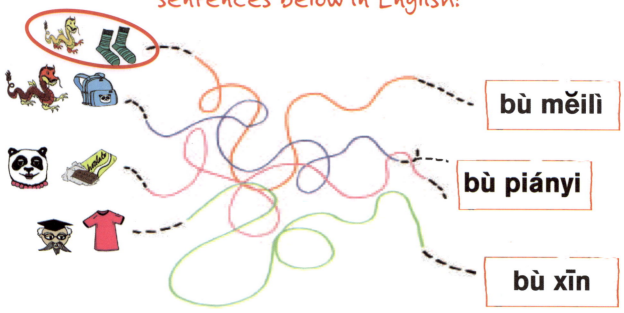

bù měilì

bù piányi

bù xīn

Xiǎolóng's socks are   **not beautiful.**

Dàlóng's bag is   the bag are not News

Mum's chocolate is   No chachret not. Yomy

Teacher's T-shirt is   the ticher not mis

How do you ask "What are you buying?" in Chinese?

Nǐ mǎi shénme?

What are you buying?

What is Dad buying?

What is Mum buying?

Wǒ mǎi hànbǎobāo.

Wǒ mǎi miàntiáo.

**I am buying
a hamburger.**

**I am buying
noodles.**

Who is buying what? Look at the panda family's
shopping list and then choose the correct answer
for the correct family members!

Dìdi	**chocolate**
Jiějie	**T-shirt**
Gēge	**shoes**
Mèimei	**mobile phone**

Younger brother   Younger sister   Older sister   Older brother

Wǒ mǎi qiǎokèlì.	Wǒ mǎi bāo.	Wǒ mǎi màozi.	Wǒ mǎi xiézi.
or	or	or	or
Wǒ mǎi miàntiáo.	Wǒ mǎi shǒujī.	Wǒ mǎi tìxùshān.	Wǒ mǎi kělè.

Let's write some new Chinese characters!

qiǎo

kè

lì

xīn

bù

mǎi

Let's play 'Battleships'! Find the Chinese characters in the grid below and say the correct reference!

	A	B	C	D	E	F
1	巧	宜	漂	很	渡	手
2	手	克	机	宜	浮	宜
3	来	漂	去	新	亮	力
4	力	好	美	宜	手	便
5	便	便	不	宜	机	亮

Ship 1 巧 **A1**

Ship 2 克 —

Ship 3 力 —

Ship 4 美 —

Ship 5 不 —

Let's write some Chinese characters! In each of the boxes you must write the correct character.

chocolate = 巧克力 new = 新 not = 不

(hěn)

What are Mum & Dad buying? Complete the boxes below and look at the 'reminder' if you have forgotten!

Mum= 妈妈 Dad= 爸爸 buy= 买 book= 书 water= 水

  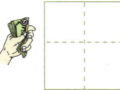

12

What have you learnt in Chapter 1?

1

shǒujī

tìxùshān

qiǎokèlì

bù

xīn

Match the correct stickers
to the Chinese words!

Congratulations, you have completed Chapter 1!

Your name: _____

Now I can...

 say *mobile phone, flowers* and *chocolate* in Chinese.

 say *new, beautiful* and *cheap* in Chinese.

 say <u>*not*</u> *new*, <u>*not*</u> *beautiful* and <u>*not*</u> *cheap* in Chinese.

 say *what I am buying* in Chinese.

 write *chocolate, new, not,* and *to buy* using characters.

Let's go and learn more Chinese in Chapter 2!

New words

jiā	house/home
wòshì	bedroom
yùshì	bathroom

More words

kètīng	sitting room
chúfáng	kitchen

Furniture

shāfā	sofa
zhuōzi	table
yǐzi	chair
chuáng	bed

Bàba zài nǎlǐ?	Where is Dad?
Bàba zài kètīng lǐ.	Dad is in the sitting room.
Chuáng zài wòshì lǐ.	The bed is in the bedroom.

Let's learn an important word in Chinese!

jiā

home/house

Let's learn how to say the rooms in my house in Chinese!

wòshì

bedroom

kètīng

sitting room

yùshì

bathroom

chúfáng

kitchen

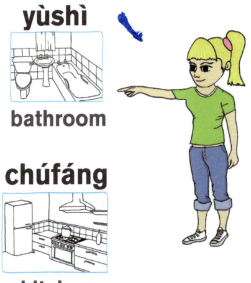

Match all the different objects to the
correct rooms in the house!

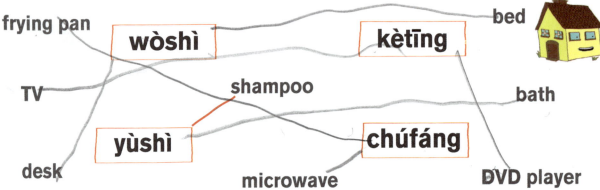

frying pan   bed

wòshì   **kètīng**

TV   shampoo   bath

yùshì   **chúfáng**

desk   microwave   DVD player

Choose your own object and write the correct room in Chinese!

Object:___wòshì___   Found in___chúfáng___

Where is Dad?

Bàba zài nǎlǐ?

Where is Dad?

Bàba zài kètīng lǐ.

Dad is in the sitting room.

Where is Mum?

Māma zài nǎlǐ?

Where is Mum?

Māma zài chúfáng lǐ.

Mum is in the kitchen.

Bàba zài nalǐ? Look at the pictures on the left and right and fill in the gaps with the correct words in Chinese!

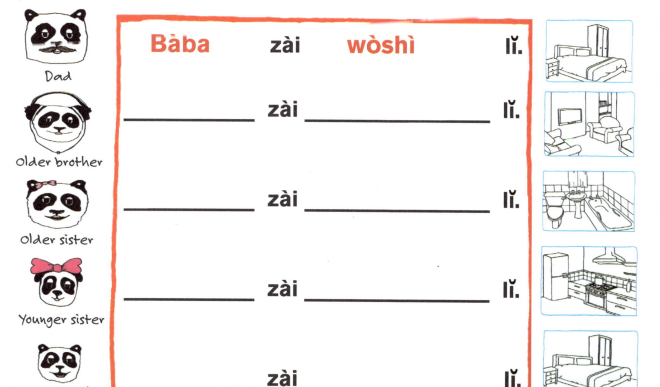

Dad	**Bàba**	**zài**	**wòshì**	**lǐ.**
Older brother	_____	zài	_____	lǐ.
Older sister	_____	zài	_____	lǐ.
Younger sister	_____	zài	_____	lǐ.
Younger brother	_____	zài	_____	lǐ.

What furniture is there in the panda family's house?

 shāfā  sofa　　**zhuōzi**  table

chuáng  bed　　**yǐzi** chair

The sofa is green! Let's play colour match! Identify the correct colours of the objects and then colour in the objects below!

	hóng	lǜ	lán	huáng	hēi
shāfā		X			
chuáng					X
yǐzi			X		
bāo				X	
zhuōzi	X				

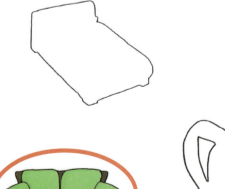

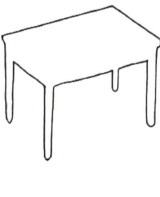

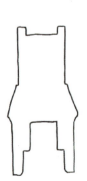

Which room is the bed in?

Chuáng zài nǎlǐ?

Chuáng zài wòshì lǐ.

**Where is
the bed?**

**The bed is
in the bedroom.**

Which room is the chair in?

Yǐzi zài nǎlǐ?

Yǐzi zài yùshì lǐ.

**Where is
the chair?**

**The chair is
in the bathroom.**

Shāfā zài nǎlǐ? Read the sentences and link the objects with the correct room.

Shāfā zài kètīng lǐ.

Yǐzi zài chúfáng lǐ.

Yǐzi zài yùshì lǐ.

Chuáng zài wòshì lǐ.

Zhuōzi zài chúfáng lǐ.

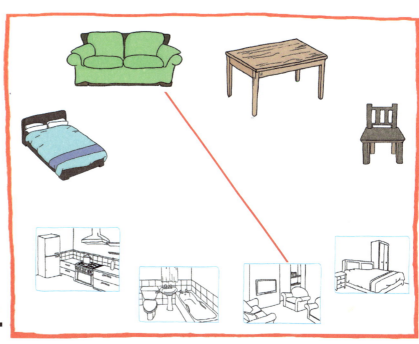

Let's write some new Chinese characters!

jiā 宀 宀 宀 宇 宇 宇 宇
家 家 家 家 家 家 家

kè 宀 宀 宀 宀 穷 突 安
客 客 客 客 客 客 客

tīng 一 厂 厂 厅 厅 厅 斤

zài 一 大 オ 在 在 在 在

shā 丶 氵 氵 氵 沙 沙 沙

fā 乙 夕 犮 发 发 发 发

How many times does 家 appear in the wordsearch? Write the number in English and then 家 in the box to the right.

沙 室 在 客 在
发 家 厅 沙 发
室 在 客 厅 家
家 沙 家 在 沙
客 客 发 客 客
在 厅 沙 沙 家
客 家 室 发 室
在 室 家 室 在
发 室 沙 发 在

How many times?

Who? Where? Look at the pictures and write the correct Chinese characters in the boxes below!

| Older brother=哥哥 | Younger sister=妹妹 | is in=在 | sitting room=客厅 |

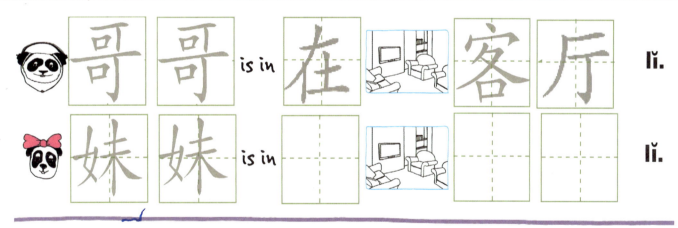

哥 哥 is in 在 客 厅 lǐ.

妹 妹 is in lǐ.

Which room is the sofa in? Look at the pictures and write the correct Chinese characters in the boxes below!

| sofa = 沙发 | hat = 帽子 | is in = 在 | bedroom = 卧室 |

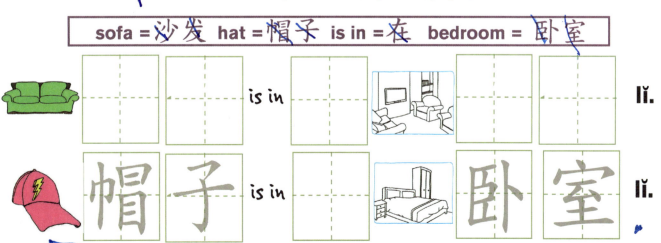

is in lǐ.

帽 子 is in 卧 室 lǐ.

What have you learnt in Chapter 2?

1	2
shǒujī	wòshì
tǐxùshān	chúfáng
qiǎokèlì	zhuōzi
bù	yǐzi
xīn	jiā

Match the correct stickers to the Chinese words!

Congratulations, you have completed Chapter 2!

Your name: _____

Now I can...

 say *house, bedroom* and *bathroom* in Chinese.

 say *sitting room* and *kitchen* in Chinese.

 say *where my family are in the house.*

 say *sofa, table, chair* and *bed* in Chinese.

 say *where the furniture is in the house.*

 write *house, sitting room, is in* and *sofa* using characters.

Let's go and learn more Chinese in Chapter 3!

Food

jīdàn	eggs
miànbāo	bread
niúròu	beef

Drink

niúnǎi	milk
chéngzhī	orange juice
píngguǒzhī	apple juice

Utensils

dāo	knife
chāzi	fork
sháozi	spoon
kuàizi	chopsticks

| Nǐmen zuò shénme? | What are you doing? |
| Wǒmen zuò fàn. | We are cooking food. |

| Tāmen zuò shénme? | What are they doing? |
| Tāmen zuò fàn. | They are cooking food. |

What is Mike eating?

jīdàn

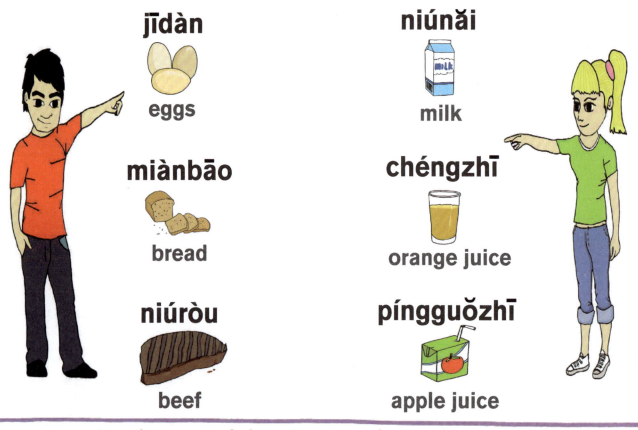

eggs

miànbāo

bread

niúròu

beef

What is Candy drinking?

niúnǎi

milk

chéngzhī

orange juice

píngguǒzhī

apple juice

What's in Mum's kitchen? Look at the crossword below and fill in our 6 new words. Also, fill in the food & drink words from Book 1!

Across

1- **hànbǎobāo**
2 - jīdàn
3 - chá
4 - kělè
5 - píngguǒzhī
6 - shuǐ
7 - miànbāo

Down

1 - chéngzhī
2 - niúnǎi
3 - pīsà
4 - qiǎokèlì
5 - niúròu

What is Dad eating?

Bàba chī shénme?

What is Dad eating?

Bàba chī niúròu.

Dad is eating beef.

What is older brother drinking?

Gēge hē shénme?

What is older brother drinking?

Gēge hē chéngzhī.

Older brother is drinking orange juice.

Bàba chī shénme? Circle the words that best match the pictures on the left.

1. Gēge / lǎoshī / jiějie / chī / hē / chéngzhī / niúròu / píngguǒzhī

2. Bàba / dìdi / Xiǎolóng / chī / hē / kělè / hànbǎobāo / miàntiáo

3. Mèimei / Dàlóng / Dìdi / chī / hē / chá / miànbāo / shuǐ / chá

4. Māma / mèimei / Mike / chī / hē / pīsà / jīdàn / hànbǎobāo

5. Jiějie / Bàba / Candy / chī / hē / miàntiáo / miànbāo / niúnǎi

What does Mum use in the kitchen?

dāo knife   **sháozi** spoon

chāzi fork   **kuàizi** chopsticks

What is this? This is a fork.

Zhè shì shénme?   **Zhè shì chāzi.**

What is this?  This is a fork.

What is that? That is a knife.

Nà shì shénme?   **Nà shì dāo.**

What is that?  That is a knife.

This is or that is? Complete the sentences by writing zhè shì or nà shì + the correct utensil in Chinese!

Zhè shì...   **Nà shì...**

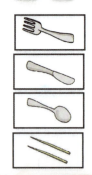

Nà   shì   chāzi.

Nà _____   shì _____   dāo _____.

Zhè _____   shì _____   shaozi _____.

Nà _____   shì _____   kuaizi _____.

How do you say to do in Chinese?

zuò

What are you doing?

Nǐmen zuò shénme?

What are
you doing?

Wǒmen zuò fàn.

We are
cooking food.

What are older sister and younger sister doing?

Tāmen zuò shénme?

What are
they doing?

Tāmen zuò fàn.

They are
cooking food.

Follow the lines to find out which **2** of our friends are cooking with Mum. Write the answers in Chinese below!

zuò fàn

Let's write some new Chinese characters!

niú

ròu

niú

nǎi

zuò

fàn

dāo

Look at the Chinese characters below and complete the missing strokes. Look, we have done one for you!

做饭牛肉

What's Xiǎolóng eating? Look at the images below and fill in the boxes with the missing Chinese characters!

eat=吃 **drink=**喝 **beef=**牛肉 **milk=** 牛奶 **hamburger=**汉堡包 **tea=**茶

 吃 做 饭

 喝

  吃 汉 堡 包

  喝 茶

What's teacher doing? Look at the images below and fill in the boxes with the missing Chinese characters!

Teacher =老师 **Younger brother =**弟弟 **Older sister =**姐姐 **cook =** 做饭

 老 师   做 饭

 弟 弟

 姐 姐

What have you learnt in Chapter 3?

1 **2** **3**

shǒujī

wòshì

jīdàn

tìxùshān

chúfáng

niúròu

qiǎokèlì

zhuōzi

niúnǎi

bù

yǐzi

chāzi

xīn

jiā

dāo

Match the correct stickers to the Chinese words!

Congratulations, you have completed Chapter 3!

Your name: _____

Now I can...

 say *egg, bread* and *beef* in Chinese.

 say *milk, orange juice* and *apple juice* in Chinese.

 say *you (plural)* and *they* in Chinese.

 say *knife, fork, spoon* and *chopsticks* in Chinese.

 write *beef, milk, cook food* and *knife* using characters.

Let's go and learn more Chinese in Chapter 4!

Subjects

Hànyǔ	Chinese
Yīngyǔ	English
shùxué	maths
kēxué	science

xuésheng a student

New words

kè	lesson
kǎoshì	exam
kèběn	textbook
zuòyè	homework

| Wǒ yǒu kèběn. | I have a textbook. |
| Wǒ méiyǒu chǐ. | I don't have a ruler. |

| Wǒ yǒu Hànyǔ kè. | I have a Chinese lesson. |
| Wǒ méiyǒu shùxué kè. | I don't have a maths lesson. |

What subjects do Dàlóng and Xiǎolóng study at school?

Hànyǔ

Chinese

Yīngyǔ

English

shùxué
maths

kēxué
science

Chinese is a-mazing! Help our friends get to their lessons! Write down the lesson names in the spaces below in Chinese!

Gēge Hànyǔ _____

Mike _Yīngyǔ_

Xiǎolóng _Shùxué_

Candy _Kēxué_

Let's learn a useful word at my school!

xuésheng  **student**

Who are you?

Nǐmen shì shéi?

Who are you?

Wǒmen shì xuésheng.

We are students.

Who are they?

Tāmen shì shéi?

Who are they?

Tāmen shì lǎoshī.

They are teachers.

Can you help Mike identify all the different people at his school? Link the questions on the left to the answers on the right.

 Nǐ shì shéi?   **Wǒmen shì lǎoshī.**

 Tā shì shéi?   **Wǒ shì lǎoshī.**

 Nǐmen shì shéi?   **Tāmen shì xuésheng.**

 Tāmen shì shéi?   **Tā shì xuésheng.**

Let's learn some more useful words at school!

 kè lesson   kèběn textbook

kǎoshì exam   zuòyè homework

Which subject?

Hànyǔ kè

Yīngyǔ kèběn

Chinese lesson   English textbook

shùxué kǎoshì

kēxué zuòyè

maths exam   science homework

It's an English textbook! Look at the pictures and write the correct words in Chinese in the spaces provided!

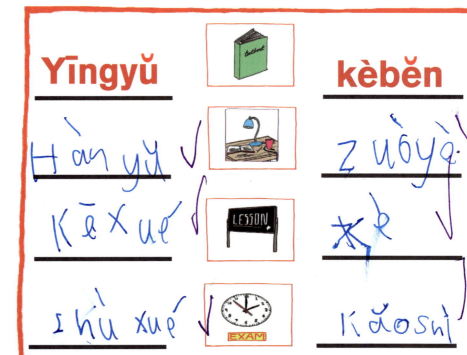

Yīngyǔ **kèběn**

Hànyǔ ✓   zuòyè ✓

Kēxué ✓   kè ✓

shùxué ✓   kǎoshì ✓

How do you say 'to have' and 'to not have' in Chinese?

 yǒu   **méiyǒu**

What do Candy and Dàlóng have and not have?

Wǒ yǒu kèběn.

I have a
textbook.

Wǒ méiyǒu chǐ.

I don't have
a ruler.

What lessons do Mike and Xiǎolóng have and not have?

Wǒ yǒu Hànyǔ kè.

 I have a
Chinese lesson.

Wǒ méiyǒu shùxué kè.

I don't have a
maths lesson.

What's in the bag? Decide if Mike has or does not have the objects below. Circle either yǒu or méiyǒu!

kèběn	yǒu	méiyǒu
qiǎokèlì	yǒu	méiyǒu
shǒujī	yǒu	méiyǒu
màozi	yǒu	méiyǒu
wàzi	yǒu	méiyǒu

Let's write some new Chinese characters!

Hàn

yǔ

kè

běn

yǒu

méi

Help Dàlóng to count how many Chinese characters there are on his textbook. Make sure you write the answer in Chinese!

Candy's got a Chinese lesson today. Complete the boxes below with the correct Chinese characters!

Chinese= 汉语   **English=**英语   **lesson=** 课   **textbook=** 课本

Fill in the boxes for **yǒu** or **méiyǒu** on the left and and the name of the object on the right - all in Chinese characters!

have=有 **don't have=**没有 **lesson=** 课 **textbook=**课本 **Chinese=**汉语

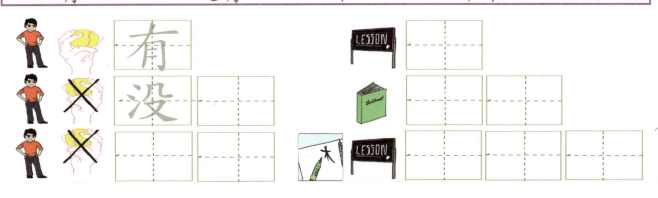

What have you learnt in Chapter 4?

1	2	3	4
shǒujī	wòshì	jīdàn	Hànyǔ
tìxùshān	chúfáng	niúròu	shùxué
qiǎokèlì	zhuōzi	niúnǎi	kèběn
bù	yǐzi	chāzi	zuòyè
xīn	jiā	dāo	xuésheng

Match the correct stickers to the Chinese words!

Congratulations, you have completed Chapter 4!

Your name: _____

Now I can...

 say *Chinese, English, Maths* and *Science* in Chinese.

 say *student* in Chinese.

 say *lesson, exam, textbook* and *homework* in Chinese.

 say *have* and *don't have* in Chinese.

 say *what lessons you have* and *don't have* in Chinese.

 write *Chinese, lesson, textbook, have* and *don't have* using characters.

Let's go and learn more Chinese in Chapter 5!

More food & drink

jīròu	chicken
shǔtiáo	chips
qìshuǐ	fizzy drinks
kāfēi	coffee

More new words

hǎochī	tasty (food)
hǎohē	tasty (drink)

Wǒ xǐhuan Zhōngguó.   I like China.
Wǒ bù xǐhuan jīròu.   I don't like chicken.

Nǐ chī shǔtiáo ma?   Are you eating chips?
Wǒ chī shǔtiáo.   I am eating chips.

Tāmen hē kāfēi ma?   Are they drinking coffee?
Tāmen bù hē kāfēi.   They are not drinking coffee.

What food and drink do Mike and Candy have in their kitchen?

jīròu

chicken

qìshuǐ

fizzy drinks

shǔtiáo

chips

kāfēi

coffee

What's older brother eating on Monday mornings? Fill in the gaps below by writing the food and drink in English.

	MORNING	AFTERNOON
MONDAY	**shǔtiáo/shuǐ**	**pīsà /qìshuǐ**
TUESDAY	**hànbǎobāo/ chá**	**jīròu / kělè**
WEDNESDAY	**niúròu / chéngzhī**	**jīròu / kāfēi**
THURSDAY	**qiǎokèlì / shuǐ**	**jīdàn / píngguǒzhī**
FRIDAY	**jīròu / niúnǎi**	**miànbāo / kělè**

Monday morning   **chips and water**

Wednesday afternoon   _chicken and coffee_

Friday morning   _chicken and milk_

Tuesday afternoon   _chicken and coke_

What food does he eat 3 times?   _chicken_

How do you say like and not like in Chinese?

 **xǐhuan   bù xǐhuan**

What does Mike and Xiǎolóng like?

Wǒ xǐhuan Zhōngguó.

I like China.

Wǒ xǐhuan chá.

I like tea.

What does Candy and teacher not like?

Wǒ bù xǐhuan jīròu.

I don't like chicken.

Wǒ bù xǐhuan kāfēi.

I don't like coffee.

What does Dàlóng like and not like?
Fill in the spaces in Chinese!

Wǒ xǐhuan...

Wǒ bù xǐhuan...

shǔtiáo

jīròu

kāfēi

Jīdàn

pīsa

kāfēi

Let's learn some more useful words!

 hǎochī tasty (food)   **bù hǎochī** not tasty (food)

 hǎohē tasty (drink)   **bù hǎohē** not tasty (drink)

Let's practise using our new words!

 **Shǔtiáo hěn hǎochī.**   **Jīròu bù hǎochī.**

 Chips
are tasty.   Chicken
is not tasty.

Qìshuǐ hěn hǎohē.   **Kāfēi bù hǎohē.**

 Fizzy drinks
are tasty.   Coffee
is not tasty.

Look at the pictures and write **tasty** or **not tasty** in Chinese in the gaps on the right!

tasty	not tasty
🍗	🥤
☕	🍟
🥩	🧃
🥤	🥚
🍞	🥛

niúròu	**hǎochī**
shǔtiáo	bu hao chi
jīròu	hao chi
jīdàn	bù hao chi
miànbāo	hǎo chī

How do you ask a question in Chinese?

ma?

Are you eating chips?

Nǐ chī shǔtiáo <u>ma</u>?

Are you eating chips?

Wǒ chī shǔtiáo.

I am eating chips.

Are they drinking coffee?

Tāmen hē kāfēi <u>ma</u>?

Are they drinking coffee?

Tāmen bù hē kāfēi.

They are not drinking coffee.

Can you help younger brother put the questions back into the correct order. Look, the first one has already been done!

ma shǔtiáo chī nǐ?	**Nǐ chī shǔtiáo ma?**
kāfēi hē tāmen ma?	hē Kafē lamimma ?
jīròu chī ma nǐmen?	_____ ?
kělè ma tā hē?	_____ ?
ma qiǎokèlì chī nǐ?	_____ ?

Let's write some new Chinese characters!

jī

鸡

ròu

肉

qì

汽

shuǐ

水

xǐ

喜

huan

欢

ma?

吗

Help Dàlóng to spot and **write** the difference between the Chinese characters on the left and the right!

鸡 肉
汽 水

鸡 肉
汽 水

Is the chicken tasty? What about the fizzy drinks?
Complete the Chinese characters in the boxes below.

chicken=鸡肉 **fizzy drinks**=汽水 **tasty** =好吃 **tasty** =好喝 **not**=不

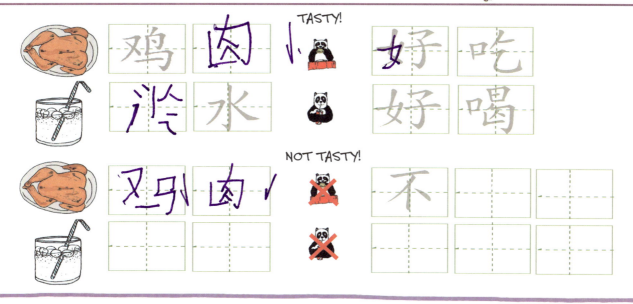

TASTY!

NOT TASTY!

Help Xiǎolóng to say what he likes and doesn't like.
Complete the Chinese characters in the boxes below!

like = 喜欢 **not** = 不 **bread**= 面包 **coffee** = 咖啡

 面

 咖 啡

What have you learnt in Chapter 5?

	1	2	3	4	5
	shǒujī	wòshì	jīdàn	Hànyǔ	jīròu
	tìxùshān	chúfáng	niúròu	shùxué	shǔtiáo
	qiǎokèlì	zhuōzi	niúnǎi	kèběn	kāfēi
	bù	yǐzi	chāzi	zuòyè	qìshuǐ
	xīn	jiā	dāo	xuésheng	xǐhuan

53

Match the correct stickers
to the Chinese words!

Congratulations, you have completed Chapter 5!

Your name:_____

Now I can...

 say *chicken, chips, coffee* and *fizzy drinks* in Chinese.

 ask a question in Chinese.

 say *tasty* and *not tasty* in Chinese.

 say what you *like* and *don't like* in Chinese.

 write *chicken, fizzy drinks, like* and the *question word* using characters.

Let's go and learn more Chinese in Chapter 6!

New words

diànshì	TV
diànnǎo	computer
diànyǐng	film

More words...

yǒu yìsi	interesting
hǎo wán	funny
wúliáo	boring

Hobbies

kàn diànshì	watch TV
kàn diànyǐng	watch a film
yòng diànnǎo	use the computer
shàng wǎng	be online

Wǒ kàn diànshì.	I am watching TV.
Wǒ kàn diànyǐng.	I am watching a film.
Bàba yòng diànnǎo.	Dad is using the computer.
Māma shàng wǎng.	Mum is online.

What's in the panda family's sitting room?

diànshì   **diànnǎo**   **diànyǐng**

TV   computer   film

What are Dàlóng's hobbies? Fill in the blanks below with either TV, computer, film and/or book in Chinese!

The Bible is a famous ___**shū**___. BOOK

Shrek is my favourite ___diànyǐng___. film

I can use the internet on a ___diànnǎo___. computer

I am watching the ___diànshì___ programme. (TV)

Harry Potter is a ___shū(book)___ and a ___diànyǐng (movie)___

Which room is the TV in?

Diànshì zài nǎlǐ?

Where is
the TV?

Diànshì zài kètīng lǐ.

The TV is
in the sitting room.

Which room is the computer in?

Diànnǎo zài nǎlǐ?

Where is
the computer?

Diànnǎo zài wòshì lǐ.

The computer is
in the bedroom.

Which room is the table in? Fill in the blanks below with the correct names of the rooms in Chinese!

 Zhuōzi zài nǎlǐ?
Zhuōzi zài chúfáng lǐ.

 **Diànshì zài nǎlǐ?**
Diànshì zài kètīng lǐ.

Yǐzi zài nǎlǐ?
Yǐzi zài _____ lǐ.

Diànnǎo zài nǎlǐ?
Diànnǎo zài _____ lǐ.

yùshì

wòshì

kètīng

chúfáng

Hey Mike, what do you think of the film?
Let's learn 3 new words!

yǒu yìsi	hǎo wán	wúliáo

interesting	funny	boring

Look at the middle pictures and decide whether to write 'interesting', 'funny' or 'boring' in Chinese!

tasty	not tasty	
🎬	🐼	**wúliáo**
📕	🐼	
🖥	🐼	
📺	🐼	

Draw pictures of 2 hobbies in the boxes and then say what you think of them in Chinese in the spaces below!

_____   _____

Let's learn 4 hobbies in Chinese!

kàn diànshì

watch TV

kàn diànyǐng

watch a film

yòng diànnǎo

use the computer

shàng wǎng

be online

What are our friends doing?

Wǒ kàn diànshì.

I am watching TV.

Wǒ kàn diànyǐng.

I am watching a film.

Bàba yòng diànnǎo.

Dad is using the computer.

Māma shàng wǎng.

Mum is online.

What are the panda family doing? Fill in the blanks with the family members and what they are doing?

 Gēge **yòng** **diànnǎo.**

 _____  **kàn** _____.

 _____ **kàn** _____.

 _____  **shàng** _____.

Let's write some new Chinese characters!

diàn

shì

hǎo

wán

kàn

Trace over the characters to complete the sentence!

Little brother= 弟弟	like= 喜欢	watch= 看	TV= 电视

弟 弟 　 喜 欢 　 看 电 视

Little brother 　 **likes** 　 **watching** 　 **TV**

TV is fun! Complete the Chinese characters on the right to say what you think of the pictures on the left!

book= 书	TV= 电视	film= 电影	fun= 好玩	boring= 无聊	interesting= 有意思

 书 　 hěn

 　 hěn 无 聊

 影 　 hěn 有 意 思

What are Dàlóng and Xiǎolóng doing? Complete the boxes below with the correct Chinese characters!

Dàlóng= 大龙	Xiǎolóng= 小龙	watch= 看	TV= 电视	film= 电影

 大 龙 　 is watching TV.  看

 小 龙 　 is watching a film.  影

What have you learnt in Chapter 6?

1	2	3	4	5
shǒujī	wòshì	jīdàn	Hànyǔ	jīròu
tìxùshān	chúfáng	niúròu	shùxué	shǔtiáo
qiǎokèlì	zhuōzi	niúnǎi	kèběn	kāfēi
bù	yǐzi	chāzi	zuòyè	qìshuǐ
xīn	jiā	dāo	xuésheng	xǐhuan

Match the correct stickers to the Chinese words!

6

diànnǎo

diànshì

diànyǐng

wúliáo

hǎo wán

Congratulations, you have completed Chapter 6!

Your name:_____

Now I can...

 say *computer, TV* and *film* in Chinese.

 say *interesting, funny* and *boring* in Chinese.

 say *read a book, use the computer* and *be online* in Chinese.

 ask someone *what they are watching* and *say what I am watching.*

 write *TV, funny* and *to watch* using characters.

Let's go and learn more Chinese in Chapter 7!

New words

pǎobù	running
zúqiú	football
yóuyǒng	swimming

More words

qiú	ball
tǐyù	P.E
bǐsài	match
yùndòng	sports

tī zúqiú	to play football
dǎ wǎngqiú	to play tennis
dǎ pīngpāngqiú	to play ping pong

Nǐ yào kàn diànshì ma?	Do you want to watch TV?
Wǒ yào kàn diànshì.	I want to watch TV.

Tāmen yào tī zúqiú ma?	Do they want to play football?
Tāmen bú yào tī zúqiú.	They don't want to play football.

Let's learn some 'sporty' words!

pǎobù

running

zúqiú

football

yóuyǒng

swimming

Dàlóng is confused! Help him to Match the 6 sports & activities to all the different items below.

shàng wǎng

eggs

football

TV

pǎobù

diving board

run/jog

yóuyǒng

zuò fàn

flour

pool

be online

sprint

video

program

film

zúqiú

kàn diànshì

goal

foul

cake

internet

Write your own activity in English and write what you think of it in Chinese! Boring, interesting or fun?

Activity:_____   **Opinion**_____

What sports do the 2 brothers like?

tī zúqiú

play football

dǎ wǎngqiú

play tennis

dǎ pīngpāngqiú

play ping pong

Candy likes playing football

Wǒ xǐhuan tī zúqiú!

I like playing football!

Mike doesn't like playing tennis!

Wǒ bù xǐhuan dǎ wǎngqiú!

I don't like playing tennis!

What sports & activities do the pandas like and not like? Look at the pictures and complete the sentences!

Gēge <u>bù</u> <u>xǐhuan</u> <u>yóuyǒng.</u>

Gēge ___ ___ ___ ___.

Gēge ___ ___ ___ ___.

Jiějie ___ ___ ___.

Jiějie ___ ___ ___.

Jiějie ___ ___ ___.

Let's learn how to say some more 'sports' words!

qiú

ball

tǐyù

P.E

bǐsài

match

yùndòng

sports

What a mix up! Look at the pictures and then write the correct Chinese name in the spaces below!

qiú _____ _____ _____

_____ _____ _____ **bǐsài**

_____ **tǐyù** _____ _____

_____ _____ _____ **yùndòng**

How do you say 'want' and 'not want' in Chinese?

 # yào   bú yào

Does little sister want to watch TV?

Nǐ yào kàn diànshì ma?

  Do you want to watch TV?

Wǒ yào kàn diànshì.

I want to watch TV.

Do Dàlóng and Xiǎolóng want to play football?

Tāmen yào tī zúqiú ma?

  Do they want to play football?

Tāmen bú yào tī zúqiú.

They don't want to play football.

What does Candy want and not want to do! Fill in the gaps with the correct sports and activities!

Wǒ yào...

Wǒ bú yào...

dǎ wǎng qiú.

_____.

_____.

_____.

_____.

_____.

_____.

Let's write some new Chinese characters!

pǎo

bù

zú

qiú

yào

Help little sister find 3 in a row! Find as many of the characters from page 70 as you can.

是 不 步 步 步 要 录 要 要 要
笔 书 球 球 球 要 厨 房 足 跑
要 要 要 黑 球 要 跑 足 跑 跑
足 足 足 姐 妹 球 足 爸 足 跑
跑 步 足 步 步 步 足 足 足 房
球 球 球 足 球 要 要 要 不 绿

What do the 2 dragons like doing? Complete the correct Chinese characters in the boxes below.

Dàlóng= 大龙 **Xiǎolóng=** 小龙 **like=** 喜欢 **run=** 跑步 **football=** 足球

Do you want to **play** football? Complete the correct Chinese characters in the boxes below.

I = 我 **You=** 你 **want=** 要 **not=** 不 **play=** 踢 **football=** 足球

I 我 踢

You 你 踢

What have you learnt in Chapter 7?

1	2	3	4	5
shǒujī	wòshì	jīdàn	Hànyǔ	jīròu
tìxùshān	chúfáng	niúròu	shùxué	shǔtiáo
qiǎokèlì	zhuōzi	niúnǎi	kèběn	kāfēi
bù	yǐzi	chāzi	zuòyè	qìshuǐ
xīn	jiā	dāo	xuésheng	xǐhuan

Match the correct stickers
to the Chinese words!

6	7			
diànnǎo	pǎobù			
diànshì	yóuyǒng			
diànyǐng	zúqiú			
wúliáo	wǎngqiú			
hǎo wán	tǐyù			

Congratulations, you have completed Chapter 7!

Your name: _____

Now I can...

- say *football*, *running* and *swimming* in Chinese.

- say *play football* and *play tennis* in Chinese.

- say that *I like* and *don't like doing sports* in Chinese.

- say *ball*, *P.E*, *match* and *sports* in Chinese.

- say *I want* and *I don't want* in Chinese.

- write *running*, *football* and *want* using characters.

Let's go and learn more Chinese in Chapter 8!

New Words

xīngqī	week
yuè	month

Week

Xīngqī yī	Monday
Xīngqī èr	Tuesday
Xīngqī sān	Wednesday
Xīngqī sì	Thursday
Xīngqī wǔ	Friday
Xīngqī liù	Saturday
Xīngqī tiān	Sunday

Months

Yī yuè	January
Èr yuè	February
Sān yuè	March
Sì yuè	April
Wǔ yuè	May
Liù yuè	June
Qī yuè	July
Bā yuè	August
Jiǔ yuè	September
Shí yuè	October
Shíyī yuè	November
Shí'èr yuè	December

Which day?

Xīngqī jǐ?	What day is it?
Xīngqī liù	It's Saturday.

Which month?

Jǐ yuè?	Which month is it?
Shí'èr yuè.	It's December.

Do you remember your numbers in Chinese?

1	yī	一	7	qī	七	
2	èr	二	8	bā	八	
3	sān	三	9	jiǔ	九	
4	sì	四	10	shí	十	
5	wǔ	五	11	shíyī	十一	
6	liù	六	12	shí'èr	十二	

What time is it? It's 11 o'clock!

Jǐ diǎn le?

Shí yī diǎn.

What time is it?

It's 11 o'clock.

Complete the correct times in Chinese inside the clock. Next, write the characters outside in the green boxes!

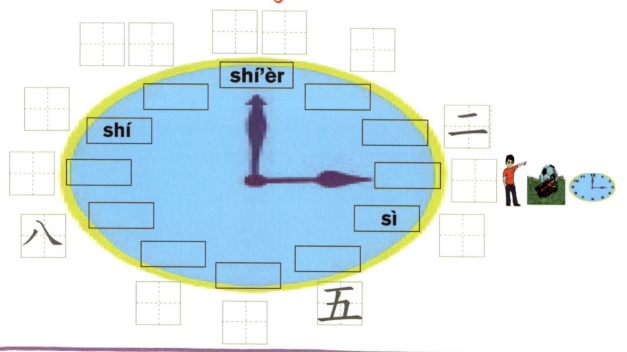

What time is Mike playing football? Answer in Chinese!

   = _____ _____

How do you say 'week' in Chinese?

Xīngqī

How do you say the 7 days of the week in Chinese?

Xīngqī yī	Monday
Xīngqī èr	Tuesday
Xīngqī sān	Wednesday
Xīngqī sì	Thursday
Xīngqī wǔ	Friday
Xīngqī liù	Saturday
Xīngqī tiān	Sunday

What's younger brother doing this week? Answer the questions below choosing the correct day in Chinese!

Xīngqī yī			
Xīngqī èr			
Xīngqī sān			
Xīngqī sì			
Xīngqī wǔ			
Xīngqī liù			
Xīngqī tiān			

On what day does little brother play ping pong? <u>Xīngqī yī</u>

On what day does little brother play tennis? _____

On what 2 days does little brother study Chinese? _____ _____

On what 2 days does little brother study maths? _____ _____

How do you say month in Chinese?

yuè

How do you say the 12 months of the year in Chinese?

Yī yuè	January	Qī yuè	July
Èr yuè	February	Bā yuè	August
Sān yuè	March	Jiǔ yuè	September
Sì yuè	April	Shí yuè	October
Wǔ yuè	May	Shí yī yuè	November
Liù yuè	June	Shí'èr yuè	December

Happy Birthday! Look at the pictures and write down in what month our friends have their birthdays in Chinese!

 February   **èr yuè** _____

 August _____

 May _____

 November _____

 April _____

 December _____

 September _____

 July _____

 October _____

 June _____

 January _____

 March _____

How do you ask what day of the week and what month it is in Chinese?

Xīngqī jǐ?   Jǐ yuè?

Which day of the week is it?

Xīngqī jǐ?

Xīngqī tiān.

Which day of the week is it?

Sunday

It's Sunday.

Which month is it?

Jǐ yuè?

Shí'èr yuè.

Which month is it?

December

It's December.

Which day of the week? Which month? Fill in the gaps with the correct day/month!

 Xīngqī jǐ? Thursday **Xīngqī sì.**

 Jǐ yuè? February _____.

 Xīngqī jǐ? Tuesday _____.

 Jǐ yuè? November _____.

Let's write some new Chinese characters!

xīng

丨　冂　冃　旦　旦　旦　旦

旱　星　星　星　星　星　星

qī

一　十　卄　艹　艹　其　其

其　刞　期　期　期　期　期

tiān
sunday

一　二　天　天　天　天　天

yuè

丿　几　月　月　月　月　月

jǐ?

丿　几　几　几　几　几　几

Help Dàlóng decide which day and which month it is. Write the answers in English in the gaps below!

星期五	**Friday**	七月	**July**
星期一	_____	十二月	_____
星期六	_____	三月	_____
星期二	_____	九月	_____

Fill in the boxes with the correct Chinese characters!

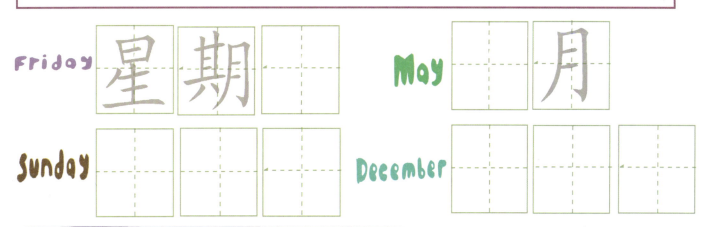

Friday= 星期五　Sunday= 星期天　May= 五月　December= 十二月

Friday 星 期 ☐

Sunday ☐ ☐ ☐

May ☐ 月

December ☐ ☐ ☐

  Which day? Which month? Fill in the boxes with the correct Chinese characters!

What day?= 星期几　Which month?= 几月　Monday= 星期一　August= 八月

☐ ☐ 几 ? Monday ☐ ☐ ☐

☐ ☐ ? August ☐ ☐

What have you learnt in Chapter 8?

1	2	3	4	5
shǒujī	wòshì	jīdàn	Hànyǔ	jīròu
tìxùshān	chúfáng	niúròu	shùxué	shǔtiáo
qiǎokèlì	zhuōzi	niúnǎi	kèběn	kāfēi
bù	yǐzi	chāzi	zuòyè	qìshuǐ
xīn	jiā	dāo	xuésheng	xǐhuan

Match the correct stickers
to the Chinese words!

6	7	8		
diànnǎo	pǎobù	xīngqīyī		
diànshì	yóuyǒng	xīngqī tiān		
diànyǐng	zúqiú	sān yuè		
wúliáo	wǎngqiú	shí'èr yuè		
hǎo wán	tǐyù	Jǐ yuè?		

Congratulations, you have completed Chapter 8!

Your name: _____

Now I can...

say what day of the week it is in Chinese.

say what month of the year it is in Chinese.

ask what of day of the week it is in Chinese.

ask what month of the year it is in Chinese.

write *week, 'tiān', Sunday, month,* and *how many* using characters.

Let's go and learn more Chinese in Chapter 9!

New words

qǐchuáng	to get up
chīfàn	to eat food
shuìjiào	to sleep

More new words

shàngxué	to start school
fàngxué	to finish school

Meals

zǎofàn	breakfast
wǔfàn	lunch
wǎnfàn	supper

Nǐ jǐ diǎn qǐchuáng?	What time do you get up?
Wǒ bā diǎn qǐchuáng.	I get up at 8 o'clock.

Tā jǐ diǎn fàngxué?	What time does he finish school?
Tā wǔ diǎn fàngxué.	He finishes school at 5 o'clock.

Let's learn some new words!

qǐchuáng

get up

chī fàn

eat food

shuìjiào

sleep

What time does Mike wake up?

Nǐ jǐ diǎn qǐchuáng?

What time
do you wake up?

Wǒ bā diǎn qǐchuáng

I wake up at
8 o'clock.

Help Xiǎolóng remember his day! Fill in the gaps with the correct times and activities in Chinese

Nǐ jǐ diǎn chī fàn? Wǒ ___ shí'èr diǎn ___ ___ chī fàn. ___.

Nǐ jǐ diǎn shuìjiào? Wǒ _____ _____.

Nǐ jǐ diǎn qǐchuáng? Wǒ _____ _____.

Nǐ jǐ diǎn tī zúqiú? Wǒ _____ _____.

Nǐ jǐ diǎn yóuyǒng? Wǒ _____  _____.

How do you say **starting** and **finishing** school in Chinese?

shàngxué   **fàngxué**

to start school   to finish school

What time does younger brother finish school?

Tā jǐ diǎn fàngxué?

Tā wǔ diǎn fàngxué.

What time does he finish school?   He finishes school at 5 o'clock.

What time does Mike finish school? Look at Mike's term timetable and complete the times below in Chinese!

Xīngqī yī
Xīngqī èr
Xīngqī sān
Xīngqī sì
Xīngqī wǔ

Monday	**Tā jǐ diǎn fàngxué?**	**Tā wǔ diǎn fàngxué.**
Tuesday	**Tā jǐ diǎn shàngxué?**	**Tā** ____ ____ **shàngxué.**
Wednesday	**Tā jǐ diǎn shàng wǎng?**	**Tā** ____ ____ **shàng wǎng.**
Thursday	**Tā jǐ diǎn chī fàn?**	**Tā** ____ ____ **chī fàn.**
Friday	**Tā jǐ diǎn kàn diànshì?**	**Tā** ____ ____ **kàn diànshì.**

zǎofàn

breakfast

wǔfàn

lunch

wǎnfàn

supper

 ## What time does Dad eat his breakfast?

Nǐ jǐ diǎn chī zǎofàn?

What time do you eat breakfast?

Wǒ qī diǎn chī zǎofàn.

I eat breakfast at 7 o'clock.

Look carefully at the pictures and match the questions on the left to the answers on the right!

1.

2.

3.

4.

5.

6.

1. **Dìdi jǐ diǎn chī zǎofàn?**

2. **Mèimei jǐ diǎn chī wǔfàn?**

3. **Gēge jǐ diǎn chī wǎnfàn?**

4. **Jiějie jǐ diǎn chī wǔfàn?**

5. **Dìdi jǐ diǎn chī wǎnfàn?**

6. **Gēge jǐ diǎn chī zǎofàn?**

Tā bā diǎn chī wǎnfàn.

Tā jiǔ diǎn chī wǎnfàn.

Tā yī diǎn chī wǔfàn.

Tā shí'èr diǎn chī wǔfàn.

Tā qī diǎn chī zǎofàn.

Tā shí diǎn chī zǎofàn.

What's for supper and breakfast?

Wǎnfàn nǐ chī shénme?

Wǎnfàn wǒ chī jīròu.

What are you
eating for supper?

I am eating chicken
for supper.

Wǔfàn nǐmen hē shénme?

Wǔfàn wǒmen hē chéngzhī.

What are you
drinking for lunch?

We are drinking
orange juice for lunch.

Mike is drinking Coca Cola for lunch! Look carefully at the pictures and fill in the blanks in the answers on the right!

 1.

3.

2.

4.

1. **Wǔfàn Mike hē shénme?**   **Wǔfàn Mike hē kělè.**

2. **Wǎnfàn Candy chī shénme?**   _____ **Candy chī** _____.

3. **Zǎofàn Xiǎolóng hē shénme?**   _____ **Xiǎolóng hē** _____.

4. **Wǎnfàn Dàlóng chī shénme?**   _____ **Dàlóng chī** _____.

Let's write some **new** Chinese characters!

qǐ

chuáng

shàng

xué

zǎo

fàn

It's time to get up! Look at the pictures, then trace and write the correct characters in the boxes below!

You= 你 What time?=几点 get up= 起床 I = 我 7 o'clock = 七点

You 你 几 点 起 床 ?

I 我 ☐ ☐  ☐ ☐ ☐

It's school time! Look at the pictures and write the matching characters in the boxes below!

You=你 What time?=几点 go to school=上学 I =我 8 o'clock =八点

You 你 ☐ ☐ 上 学 ?

I 我 ☐ ☐ ☐ ☐ ☐

What are Mike and Candy eating for breakfast? Complete the Chinese characters in the boxes below!

Breakfast= 早饭 He= 他 She= 她 eat= 吃 bread= 面包 eggs= 鸡蛋

 早 饭 He 他 吃 面 包

 ☐ ☐ She 她 喝 鸡 蛋

What have you learnt in Chapter 9?

1	2	3	4	5
shǒujī	wòshì	jīdàn	Hànyǔ	jīròu
tìxùshān	chúfáng	niúròu	shùxué	shǔtiáo
qiǎokèlì	zhuōzi	niúnǎi	kèběn	kāfēi
bù	yǐzi	chāzi	zuòyè	qìshuǐ
xīn	jiā	dāo	xuésheng	xǐhuan

Match the correct stickers to the Chinese words!

6	7	8	9
diànnǎo	pǎobù	Monday xīngqīyī	qǐchuáng
diànshì	yóuyǒng	sunday xīngqī tiǎn	shuìjiào
diànyǐng	zúqiú	March sān yuè	zǎofàn
wúliáo	wǎngqiú	December shí'èr yuè	wǔfàn
hǎo wán	tǐyù	Jǐ yuè?	wǎnfàn

Congratulations, you have completed Chapter 9!

Your name: _____

Now I can...

- say *get up, eat food* and *sleep* in Chinese.

- say *what time* I get up, eat food and sleep in Chinese.

- say *go to school* and *finish school* in Chinese.

- say *breakfast, lunch* and *supper* in Chinese.

- say *what time* and *what I eat* for breakfast, lunch and supper in Chinese.

- write *get up, go to school* and *breakfast* using characters.

Let's go and learn more Chinese in Chapter 10!

New words

jiàqī	holidays
hǎi	sea
hǎitān	beach
fàndiàn	hotel

Places in China

Shànghǎi	Shanghai
Xiāng Gǎng	Hong Kong
Huáng Hé	Yellow River

Places in Beijing

Gùgōng	Forbidden City
Cháng Chéng	Great Wall of China
Tiān'ānmén	Heaven's Gate

Nǐ qù nǎlǐ?	Where are you going?
Wǒ qù Shànghǎi.	I am going to Shanghai.

Nǐmen qù nǎlǐ?	Where are you going?
Wǒmen qù Gùgōng.	We are going to the Forbidden City.

Let's learn some new holiday words.

jiàqī

holidays

hǎitān

beach

hǎi

sea

fàndiàn

hotel

Help Candy to find all the words above + all the countries and cities that we learnt in Book 1!

 Zhōngguó

 Měiguó

 jiàqī

 hǎitān

 Běijīng

 Yīngguó

 Fǎguó

 hǎi

 fàndiàn

 Lúndūn

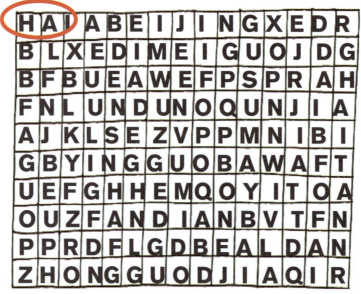

Let's learn more names of places in China!

Shànghǎi  **Shanghai**

Xiāng Gǎng  **Hong Kong**

Huáng Hé  **Yellow River**

Does Dad like Hong Kong?

Nǐ xǐhuan Xiāng Gǎng ma?

Do you like Hong Kong?

Wǒ xǐhuan Xiāng Gǎng!

I like Hong Kong!

Candy doesn't like Hong Kong! Look carefully at the pictures and fill in the blanks in the questions and answers below!

1.

3.

2.

4.

1. **Candy xǐhuan Xiāng Gǎng ma?**   **Candy bù xǐhuan Xiāng Gǎng.**

2. Candy xǐhuan _____ ma?   Candy _____ Lúndūn.

3. Candy xǐhuan _____ ma?   Candy ____ _____ Shànghǎi.

4. Candy xǐhuan _____ ____ma?   Candy _____ Huáng Hé.

Let's visit the home of the Chinese Emperors!

Gùgōng

Forbidden City

Let's visit the longest wall in the world!

Cháng Chéng

The Great Wall

Let's visit the most important gate in Beijing!

Tiān'ānmén

Heaven's Gate

How do you say to go in Chinese?
qù

Where is Candy going?

Nǐ qù nǎlǐ?

Where are you going?

Wǒ qù Shànghǎi.

I am going to Shanghai.

Where are the teachers going?

Nǐmen qù nǎlǐ?

Where are you going?

Wǒmen qù Gùgōng.

We are going to the Forbidden City.

Follow the trail of all our friends and answer the questions below in Chinese!

Xiǎolóng qù nǎlǐ?
qù **Cháng Chéng.**

Gēge qù nǎlǐ?

qù _____ _____.

Dàlóng qù nǎlǐ?

qù _____ _____.

Mike qù nǎlǐ?

qù _____.

Let's write some new Chinese characters!

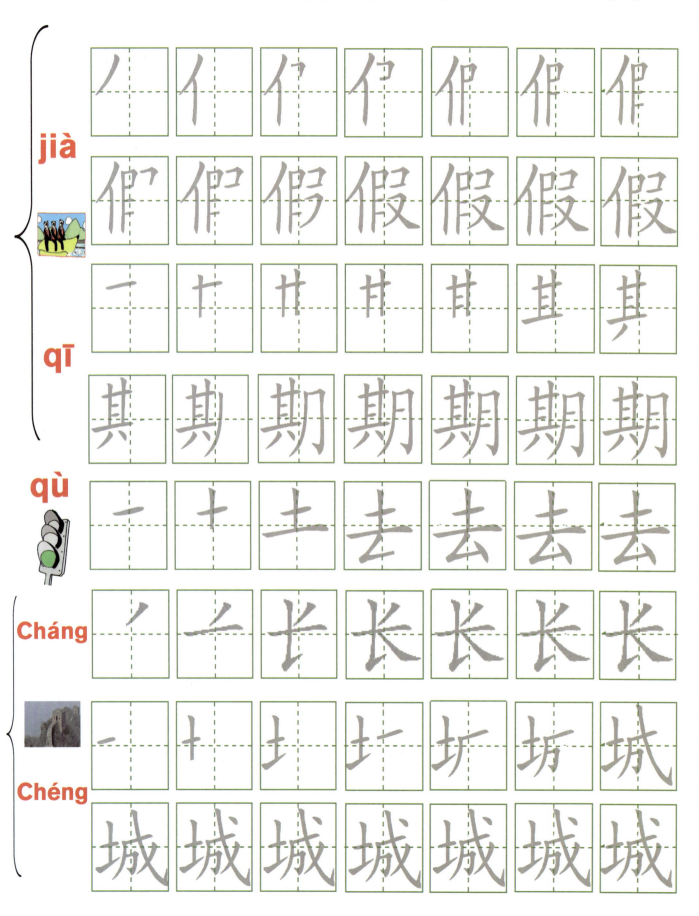

jià 假

qī 期

qù 去

Cháng 长

Chéng 城

Pair match! Find the pairs 长城 on the wall!

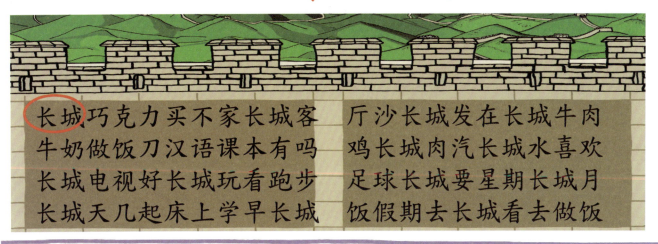

长城巧克力买不家长城客　厅沙长城发在长城牛肉
牛奶做饭刀汉语课本有吗　鸡长城肉汽长城水喜欢
长城电视好长城玩看跑步　足球长城要星期长城月
长城天几起床上学早长城　饭假期去长城看去做饭

Dàlóng is going to Shanghai! Write the matching characters in the boxes below!

Dàlóng= 大龙　Xiǎolóng= 小龙　go=去　Shanghai=上海　Hong Kong= 香港

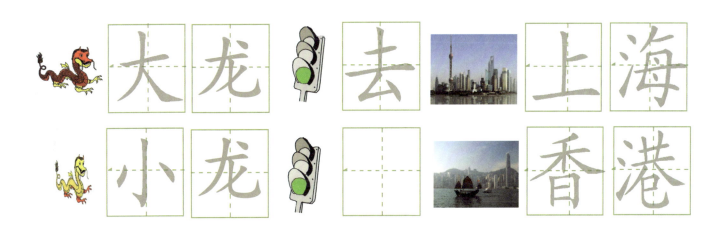

Where are the panda family going? Complete the Chinese characters in the boxes below!

They 🐼🐼 = 他们　They 🐼🐼 = 她们　go=去　Great Wall of China=长城

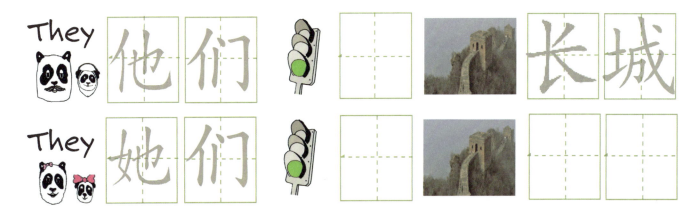

What have you learnt in Chapter 10?

1	2	3	4	5
shǒujī	wòshì	jīdàn	Hànyǔ	jīròu
tìxùshān	chúfáng	niúròu	shùxué	shǔtiáo
qiǎokèlì	zhuōzi	niúnǎi	kèběn	kāfēi
bù	yǐzi	chāzi	zuòyè	qìshuǐ
xīn	jiā	dāo	xuésheng	xǐhuan

Match the correct stickers to the Chinese words!

6	7	8	9	10
diànnǎo	pǎobù	Monday xīngqīyī	qǐchuáng	jiàqī
diànshì	yóuyǒng	Sunday xīngqī tiǎn	shuìjiào	hǎi
diànyǐng	zúqiú	March sān yuè	zǎofàn	hǎitān
wúliáo	wǎngqiú	December shí'èr yuè	wǔfàn	fàndiàn
hǎo wán	tǐyù	Jǐ yuè?	wǎnfàn	Cháng Chéng

Congratulations, you have completed Chapter 10!

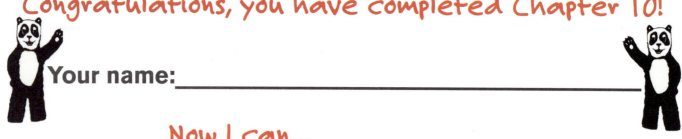

Your name: _____

Now I can...

say *holidays, sea, beach* and *hotel* in Chinese.

say *Shanghai, Hong Kong* and *Yellow River* in Chinese.

say *Forbidden City, Great Wall of China* and *Heaven's Gate* in Chinese.

say *to go* and to say *where you are going* in Chinese.

write *holiday, to go* and *Great Wall of China* using characters.

Congratulations, you have completed Book 2!

QUICK SEARCH

MORE FOOD & DRINK

qiǎokèlì	chocolate	**niúnǎi**	milk
jīdàn	eggs	**chéngzhī**	orange juice
miànbāo	bread	**píngguǒzhī**	apple juice
niúròu	beef	**qìshuǐ**	fizzy drinks
jīròu	chicken	**kāfēi**	coffee
shǔtiáo	chips		

TASTY/ NOT TASTY

hǎochī	tasty (food)	**bù hǎochī**	not tasty (food)
hǎohē	tasty (drink)	**bù hǎohē**	not tasty (drink)

DESCRIBING WORDS

xīn	new
měilì	beautiful
piányi	cheap
yǒu yìsi	interesting
hǎo wán	funny
wúliáo	boring

WHAT'S IN MY HOUSE?

shǒujī	mobile phone	**shāfā**	sofa
tǐxùshān	T-shirt	**zhuōzi**	table
chuáng	bed	**yǐzi**	chair

MY HOBBIES

diànshì	TV	**kàn diànshì**	watch TV
diànnǎo	computer	**kàn diànyǐng**	watch a film
diànyǐng	film	**yòng diànnǎo**	use the computer
		shàng wǎng	be online

SPORTS

pǎobù	running	**qiú**	ball
zúqiú	football	**tǐyù**	P.E
yóuyǒng	swimming	**bǐsài**	match
		yùndòng	sports

tī zúqiú	to play football
dǎ wǎngqiú	to play tennis
dǎ pīngpāngqiú	to play ping-pong

MY HOUSE

jiā	house/home	**shāfā**	sofa
wòshì	bedroom	**zhuōzi**	table
yùshì	bathroom	**yǐzi**	chair
kètīng	sitting room	**chuáng**	bed
chúfáng	kitchen		

HOLIDAY WORDS

jiàqī	holidays
hǎi	sea
hǎitān	beach

PLACES IN CHINA

Shànghǎi	Shanghai
Xiāng Gǎng	Hong Kong
Huáng Hé	Yellow River
Gùgōng	Forbidden City
Cháng Chéng	Great Wall
Tiān'ānmén	Heaven's Gate

WHAT'S IN THE KITCHEN?

dāo	knife	sháozi	spoon
chāzi	fork	kuàizi	chopsticks

SCHOOL STUFF

Hànyǔ	Chinese	kè	lesson
Yīngyǔ	English	kǎoshì	exam
shùxué	Maths	kèběn	textbook
kēxué	Science	xuésheng	student
		zuòyè	homework

NEGATIVES

bù xīn	not new	bù xǐhuan	don't like
bù měilì	not beautiful	bú yào	don't want
bù piányi	not cheap		

WEEKS & MONTHS

xīngqī	week	**Xīngqī jǐ?**	**What day is it?**
yuè	month	**Jǐ yuè?**	**Which month is it?**

Xīngqī yī	Monday	**Yī yuè**	January
Xīngqī èr	Tuesday	**Èr yuè**	February
Xīngqī sān	Wednesday	**Sān yuè**	March
Xīngqī sì	Thursday	**Sì yuè**	April
Xīngqī wǔ	Friday	**Wǔ yuè**	May
Xīngqī liù	Saturday	**Liù yuè**	June
Xīngqī tiān	Sunday	**Qī yuè**	July
		Bā yuè	August
		Jiǔ yuè	September
		Shí yuè	October
		Shíyī yuè	November
		Shí'èr yuè	December

January
February
March

Monday
Tuesday
Wednesday

MY DAY

qǐchuáng	to get up	**shàngxué**	to start school
chīfàn	to eat food	**fàngxué**	to finish school
shuìjiào	to sleep	**zǎofàn**	breakfast
wǔfàn	lunch	**wǎnfàn**	supper

NEW VERBS

zuò	to do	**yào**	to want
zuò fàn	to cook	**qù**	to go
xǐhuan	to like		

sunday

December

 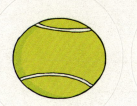     

   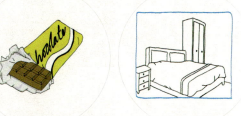